D0064768

Promises To Keep

'. . . to make gentle the life of the world.'

ROBERT F. KENNEDY:

PROMISES TO KEEP

Memorable Writings and Statements

With an Introductory Note by Edward M. Kennedy

Selected by Arthur Wortman

and Richard Rhodes

HALLMARK EDITIONS

Excerpts from *To Seek a Newer World* by Robert F. Kennedy Copyright © 1967 by Robert F. Kennedy. Reprinted by permission of Doubleday & Company, Inc. Excerpts from pp. 200, 205-6, 187 *Just Friends and Brave Enemies* by Robert F. Kennedy Copyright © 1962 by Robert F. Kennedy. Reprinted by permission of Harper & Row, Publishers.

Photographs: opposite title page by Henry Grossman © 1968 by Transworld Feature Syndicate, Inc. On pp. 12, 20, 29, 37 by Henry Grossman © 1968 by Transworld Feature Syndicate, Inc. On pp. 4, 56 © 1966 by Transworld Feature Syndicate, Inc. On p. 45 by Bill Eppridge, Life Magazine, © 1968 by Time Inc. On p. 52 by George Silk, Life Magazine, © 1968 by Time Inc.

Copyright © 1969 by Hallmark Cards Inc., Kansas City, Missouri. All Rights Reserved. Printed in the United States of America. Library of Congress Catalog Card Number: 69-17877. Standard Book Number: 87529-008-6.

PROMISES TO KEEP

Robert F. Kennedy [1925—1968]

FOREWORD

LAST YEAR, my brother Bob wrote the Foreword for the Hallmark book *John F. Kennedy: Words to Remember.* In that Foreword, he said that President Kennedy's words gave us the "tones of those struggles—for peace, for civil rights, for a better life for our people—whose echoes move us still, and shall always remain our concern."

In the selections from Robert Kennedy's writings and statements which appear in this Hallmark book, the force of his own concern for these same struggles is plainly apparent. So are his compassion for the poor and the weak, his kinship with youth and their battles to raise individual dignity, and above all, his belief in the urgency of getting on with the work of peace.

My brother believed, as he said, that "the work of our own hands, matched to reason and principle, will determine destiny." This book reflects through his own words and thoughts the course his principles and reasoning charted.

Boston, Massachusetts / November, 1968

EDWARD M. KENNEDY

Robert F. Kennedy

'*PROMISES TO KEEP*'
*Robert Kennedy introduced a memorial motion
picture about his late brother John's life to the 1964
Democratic National Convention
with these remarks:*

WHEN I think of President Kennedy I think of what
Shakespeare said in *Romeo and Juliet:*
When he shall die
Take him and cut him out in little stars
And he will make the face of heaven so fine
That all the world will be in love with night
And pay no worship to the garish sun.
President Kennedy once said that we have the capacity
to make this the best generation in the history of man-
kind or make it the last. If we do our duty, if we meet
our obligations and our responsibilities . . . in our local
cities and towns and farms, in our states and in the
country as a whole, then this country is going to be the
best generation in the history of mankind.

And I think that we must dedicate ourselves as he
frequently did to all of you when he spoke, when he
quoted from Robert Frost, when he said that which he

applied to himself but which we could apply to all of us as individuals, that "the woods are lovely, dark, and deep/But I have promises to keep,/And miles to go before I sleep,/And miles to go before I sleep."

Atlantic City, August 28, 1964

THE IDEAL OF FREEDOM
The rights and responsibilities of freedom were among Robert Kennedy's continuing concerns; he spoke of them often and with eloquence:

THE IDEAL of freedom has traveled a long and hard road through human history. Yet the record shows that the ideal persists and has an explosive power greater than that locked up within the atom. It shows that this ideal is the strongest motive of human action—that it fortifies the human will in the face of adversity and force and terror—and that the passion for equal rights for all is the ultimate weapon in the struggle for independence and human dignity.

DEMOCRACY IS never a final achievement. It is by nature an ever-changing challenge, a call to untiring effort, to renewed dedication, to new goals to meet the needs of each new generation.

We know full well the faults of our democracy—the handicaps of freedom—the inconvenience of dissent. But I know of no American who would not rather be a servant in the imperfect house of freedom, than be a master of all the empires of tyranny.

Today we face a double challenge: achievement of our ideals at home and maintenance of our leadership among the free people around the world. Are not these two challenges really one?

THE FUTURE does not belong to those who are content with today, apathetic toward common problems and their fellow man alike, timid and fearful in the face of new ideas and bold projects. Rather it will belong to those who can blend passion, reason, and courage in a personal commitment to the ideals and great enterprises of American society. It will belong to those who see that wisdom can only emerge from the clash of contending views, the passionate expression of deep and hostile beliefs. Plato said: "A life without criticism is not worth living."

This is the seminal spirit of American democracy. . . . It is this which is the hope of our nation.

A NATION . . . must work its own evolution in its own way and at its own pace. Time and tide have favored ours. The best hope we can have perhaps is that governments may listen to the voices of their people— American governments have tried to do that. We have found that when people find a willing ear they are more disposed to lend a willing hand. We think with Jefferson that our government is "The world's best hope;

the only one where every man at the call of the law would fly to the standard of the law and would meet invasions of the public order as his own personal concern."

It Is not enough to allow dissent. We must demand it. For there is much to dissent from. . . .

Yet we must, as thinking men, distinguish between the right of dissent and the way we choose to exercise that right. . . . That dissent which consists simply of sporadic and dramatic acts sustained by neither continuing labor or research—that dissent which seeks to demolish while lacking both the desire and direction for rebuilding, that dissent which, contemptuously or out of laziness, casts aside the practical weapons and instruments of change and progress—that kind of dissent is merely self-indulgence. It is satisfying, perhaps, to those who make it.

But it will not solve the problems of our society. It will not assist those seriously engaged in the difficult and frustrating work of the nation. And, when it is all over, it will not have brightened or enriched the life of a single portion of humanity in a single part of the globe.

We Live in a free and open society; that is where our strength and greatness lies. We do not hide our faults behind a wall; we do not try to bury our mistakes; we do not conceal incidents, even though they are shameful. We have no secrets from ourselves or from others. If there is an outbreak of violence in some section of the United States, it is flashed around the world in less than an hour and quickly finds its way into the Communist propaganda mill. . . .

The fact that free men persist in the search for truth is the essential difference between Communism and Democracy. The other road might appear at times to be easier—to be less troublesome—to be more immediately profitable. Our way is more difficult and in these days more perilous. The fact, however, that we would rather live in an open society than hide our troubles and mistakes behind a wall or barbed wire, is evidence of the strength of our Government and our way of life.

PEACE AMID DIVERSITY
Robert Kennedy's foreign policy goals reflected a proud but liberal view of America's role in world affairs:

THE PEACE we seek [is not] simply the absence of armed conflict or hostile division. It is the creation among nations of a web of unity, woven from the strands of economic interdependence, political cooperation, and a mounting flow of people and ideas.

OURS IS the strength of a positive faith; we need neither to hate nor fear our adversaries.

'Each generation makes its own accounting to its children.'

It Is not given to us to right every wrong, to make perfect all the imperfections of the world. But neither is it given to us to sit content in our storehouses—dieting while others starve, buying eight million new cars a year while most of the world goes without shoes. We are simply not doing enough.

I Believe that we are ready to recognize that foreign aid is not a "giveaway"—rather that it is both a moral obligation to fellow human beings and a sound and necessary investment in the future. We are incomparably richer than any other nation, now or in the history of mankind; our wealth is as great as that of all the rest of the noncommunist world put together. I believe we are ready to use this wealth for the benefit of all men. And I believe we are ready to recognize that millions saved now can mean billions lost five or ten or twenty years from now and that the human cost of delay is incalculable. Time after time, in these uncertain and dangerous years, we have reaped the consequences of neglect and delay, of misery and disease and hunger left too long to fester unremedied—in Cuba, in the Dominican Republic, in Vietnam. As President Kennedy said: "If we cannot help the many who are poor, we cannot save the few who are rich."

All Of us are most concerned about the kind of America we want to pass on to our children. Every generation inherits a world it never made; and, as it does so, it automatically becomes the trustee of that world for those who come after. In due course, each generation makes its own accounting to its children.

When our time comes, we want to make sure that we bequeath to our descendants a better and safer world than the one in which we live today—a world in which people will be free from the terrors of war and oppression, free from the handicaps of ignorance and poverty, free to realize their own talents and fulfill their own destiny.

This is the object of our foreign policy. . . .

THE RESOURCES of the earth and the ingenuity of man can provide abundance for all—so long as we are prepared to recognize the diversity of mankind and the variety of ways in which people will seek national fulfillment. This is our vision of the world—diversity of states, each developing according to its own traditions and its own genius, each solving its economic and political problems in its own manner, and all bound together by a respect for the rights of others, by a loyalty to the world community and by a faith in the dignity and responsibility of man.

We have no intention of trying to remake the world in our image, but we have no intention either of permitting any other state to remake the world in its image.

In the unending battle between diversity and dogmatism, between tolerance and tyranny, let no one mistake the American position. We deeply believe that humanity is on the verge of an age of greatness, and we do not propose to let the possibilities of that greatness be overwhelmed by those who would lock us all into the narrow cavern of a dark and rigid system. We will defend our faith by affirmation, by argument and if necessary—and heaven forbid that it should become necessary—by arms. It is our willingness to die for our ideals that makes it possible for those ideals to live. . . . Freedom means not only the *opportunity* to know but the *will* to know. That *will* can make for understanding and tolerance, and ultimately friendship and peace.

THE WIT OF ROBERT F. KENNEDY

In the 1960 Presidential race, Joey Gallo, a notorious Brooklyn underworld figure, offered to use his power to help the campaign for John Kennedy. Replied R.F.K.: Just tell everybody you're voting for Nixon.

In 1962, at the dedication of a new law school building at the University of San Francisco: I am advisedly aware that you have spent two long days now celebrating your law school's golden anniversary. I suspect that the greatest virtue in any more oratory will be in its blessed brevity. If I had any doubts on this score, Father Callahan's letter of invitation delicately enlightened me. He mentioned that Father Connoly was recovering from a spinal disc operation and also that the affair did not have to last too long. I am not clear whether he was whispering a hint, a hope, or a prayer. . . . But I'll try to keep in mind that any old place in a speech is a wonderful place to stop. I would not want any speech- induced discomfort of Father Connoly to become a widespread affliction of this assemblage.

During his 1962 visit to Japan: I had seaweed for breakfast today. To tell you the honest-to-goodness truth, it didn't taste too bad. When I went to Central Asia with Justice Douglas in 1955, they brought in a goat, very dead, plucked out its eyes, and served them to us. Justice Douglas turned to me and said, "For the sake of America, Bob, make like it's an oyster!" So things have gone up since then.

On his visit to Rome in 1962: We had a friendly audience with Pope John. He is an impressive man with wonderful humility and a fine sense of humor. He blessed us all, including the American newspapermen who were traveling with us, most of whom were not Catholics. He assured them that it was just a little blessing and wouldn't do them any harm.

To a graduating class at Marquette University: Years ago, I was a hardworking lawyer making $4,200 a year. I took my work home every night and was very diligent. Ten years later I became the Attorney General of the United States. So, you see, if you want to become successful, just get your brother elected President.

At a 1961 "Dinner of Champions": Standing here, surrounded by so many athletes, I feel I ought to present my credentials. I come from a family that has always emphasized and enjoyed sports—golf, tennis, football, baseball, and the rest. Last year, for instance, we did considerable running.

Asked if having a brother who was President were not a problem for him at times, Kennedy replied: I don't find it so. It might be for him, but it isn't for me.

At a 1962 address to the American Booksellers Association on U.S. technical publications: Incidentally, we in the government are sometimes accused of being unimaginative. I was interested to find out that one of the Government Printing Office pamphlets on the technicalities of growing tomatoes is entitled, "Hot Beds and Cold Frames." That title should do well in any market.

Campaigning for the position of U.S. Senator from New York: A few months ago while I was having breakfast with my wife, I was reading in the papers that California had replaced New York as the number-one state in population—so I turned to my wife and I said, "What can we *do*?" So I moved to New York, and in just one day I increased the population by ten and a half—my opponent has just sixty days to match that record.

While inspecting the Hudson River, notorious for its pollution, Kennedy remarked: If you fall into this river, you won't drown—you'll decay.

At an enthusiastic welcome in Jamestown, N.Y., R.F.K. quipped: I see my Long Island accent got you.

After his Senate victory, Kennedy joked in a speech about the charges of "carpetbagging" used against him: I can't tell you how happy I am to be here representing the great state of . . . ah . . . ah. . . .

At a Baseball Writers' dinner in 1965: Since my election, I've received many invitations for speaking engagements. . . . It seems they want me to speak everywhere but on the floor of the Senate. . . .

Let me say that I did not run for the Senate to become Commissioner of Baseball. I'm not interested in the position because it doesn't have enough power.

In 1965 R.F.K. scaled the difficult heights of Canada's Mt. Kennedy, named after his late brother: I remembered my mother's last words to me: "Don't slip, dear," and the admonition of a friend who had obviously never climbed: "Don't look down." And I remembered what my son, Joe, said on the telephone as I was about

to leave Seattle: "Good luck, Daddy. You'll need it."
And the reporter from a national newspaper covering
the climb told me before I began that his paper had just
completed my obituary.

*Preparing for a family trip, R.F.K. lined up his many
children and told them:* We're all going to a convention—now be good. I have something for the one who's
best. . . . And one more thing—I'll *also* have something
for the one who's worst.

Before a Women's Press Club dinner in 1965: I want to
assure you that I have no Presidential aspirations—nor
does my wife, Ethel Bird.

Speaking about campaign expenses: The cost of campaigning has become so high that to make a candidate
and his views well enough known in a state like California or New York is impossible without either a well-
known personality or enormous sums of money. As an
unknown virtually without funds, I was of course an
exception.

During the 1964 presidential campaign: General Eisen-
hower says that he could *live* with a Goldwater Administration. Well, I suppose he'd have as good a chance as
anyone else.

Asked, during the 1968 campaign, at Sioux Falls, S.D.,

'An unknown [candidate] virtually without funds. . . .'

what priority he would give to the Sioux Falls economy if elected President, R.F.K. replied: Top priority. Just this morning at breakfast I said to Ethel, "We've got to do something about the Sioux Falls economy."

Campaigning in an open car during a rainstorm: You know, I'm not sure I'd vote for a man who didn't have sense enough to come in out of the rain.

R.F.K. engaged in this dialogue with a friendly crowd in Elkhart, Indiana in 1968: "Are you going to go out and vote for me Tuesday?"

"Yes!" the crowd roared.

"And are you all going to go out and ring doorbells and tell your neighbors to vote for me?"

"Yes, Yes!" the crowd roared again.

"And have you all read my book, *To Seek a Newer World?*"

"Yes, Yes!" the crowd roared yet again.

"You lie in Elkhart, Indiana!"

Arriving in California after his unexpected defeat in the Oregon primary, Kennedy joked: I'm delighted to be here in California. I came here from Nebraska.

'THE WORK OF OUR HANDS'

*In this majestic speech, delivered to South African
and American students on two different occasions,
Robert Kennedy must have come close to the heart
of his philosophy. Certainly it is a stirring
and provocative statement:*

IF YOU fly in a plane over Europe, toward Africa or
Asia, in a few hours you will cross over oceans and
countries that have been a crucible of human history.
In minutes you will trace the migration of men over
thousands of years; seconds, the briefest glimpse, and
you will pass battlefields on which millions of men once
struggled and died. You will see no national boundaries,
no vast gulfs or high walls dividing people from people; only nature and the works of man—homes and
factories and farms—everywhere reflecting man's common effort to enrich his life. Everywhere new technology and communications bring men and nations closer
together, the concerns of one more and more becoming
the concerns of all. And our new closeness is stripping
away the false masks, the illusion of difference that is
at the root of injustice and hate and war. Only earth-
bound man still clings to the dark and poisoning super-
stition that his world is bounded by the nearest hill, his
universe ended at river shore, his common humanity
enclosed in the tight circle of those who share his town
and views and the color of his skin.

Each nation has different obstacles and different

goals, shaped by the vagaries of history and experience. Yet as I talk to young people around the world I am impressed not by the diversity but by the closeness of their goals, their desires and concerns and hope for the future. There is discrimination in New York, apartheid in South Africa and serfdom in the mountains of Peru. People starve in the streets of India; intellectuals go to jail in Russia; thousands are slaughtered in Indonesia; wealth is lavished on armaments everywhere. There are differing evils, but they are the common works of man. They reflect the imperfection of human justice, the inadequacy of human compassion, the defectiveness of our sensibility toward the sufferings of our fellows; they mark the limit of our ability to use knowledge for the well-being of others. And therefore, they call upon common qualities of conscience and of indignation, a shared determination to wipe away the unnecessary sufferings of our fellow human beings at home and around the world.

'To Rely on Youth'

Our answer is the world's hope; it is to rely on youth—not a time of life but a state of mind, a temper of the will, a quality of the imagination, a predominance of courage over timidity, of the appetite for adventure over the love of ease. The cruelties and obstacles of this swiftly changing planet will not yield to obsolete dogmas and outworn slogans. It cannot be moved by those who cling to a present that is already dying, who prefer the illusion of security to the excitement and danger that come with even the most peaceful progress. It is a revolutionary world we live in; and this generation, at home and around the world, has had thrust upon it a greater burden of responsibility than any nation that has ever lived.

"There is," said an Italian philosopher, "nothing more difficult to take in hand, more perilous to conduct, or more uncertain in its success than to take the lead in the introduction of a new order of things." Yet this is the measure of the task of this generation, and the road is strewn with many dangers.

First is the danger of futility, the belief that there is nothing one man or one woman can do against the enormous array of the world's ills—against misery and ignorance, injustice and violence. Yet many of the world's great movements, of thought and action, have flowed from the work of a single man. A young monk began the Protestant Reformation, a young general extended an empire from Macedonia to the borders of the earth, and a young woman reclaimed the territory of France. It was a young Italian explorer who discovered the New World, and the thirty-two-year-old Thomas Jefferson who proclaimed that all men are created equal. "Give me a place to stand," said Archimedes, "and I will move the world."

These men moved the world, and so can we all. Few will have the greatness to bend history itself, but each of us can work to change a small portion of events, and in the total of all those acts will be written the history of this generation. Thousands of Peace Corps volunteers are making a difference in isolated villages and city slums in dozens of countries. Thousands of unknown men and women in Europe resisted the occupation of the Nazis and many died, but all added to the ultimate strength and freedom of their countries. It is from numberless diverse acts of courage and belief that human history is shaped. Each time a man stands up for an ideal, or acts to improve the lot of others, or strikes out against injustice, he sends forth a tiny ripple of hope, and crossing each other from a million different centers of energy and daring, those ripples build a current that can sweep down the mightiest walls of oppression and resistance.

"If Athens shall appear great to you," said Pericles, "consider then that her glories were purchased by valiant men, and by men who learned their duty." That is the source of all greatness in all societies, and it is the key to progress in our time.

The second danger is that of expediency, of those who say that hopes and beliefs must bend before immediate necessities. Of course, if we would act effectively we must deal with the world as it is. We must get things done. But if there was one thing President Kennedy stood for that touched the most profound feelings of people across the world, it was the belief that idealism, high aspirations, and deep convictions are not incompatible with the most practical and efficient of programs—that there is no basic inconsistency between ideals and realistic possibilities, no separation between the deepest desires of heart and mind and the rational application of human effort to human problems. It is not realistic or hardheaded to solve problems and take action unguided by ultimate moral aims and values. It is thoughtless folly. For it ignores the realities of human faith and passion and belief, forces ultimately more powerful than all the calculations of economists and generals. Of course, to adhere to standards, to idealism, to vision in the face of immediate dangers, takes great courage and self-confidence. But we also know that only those who dare to fail greatly can ever achieve greatly.

It is this new idealism that is also, I believe, the common heritage of a generation that has learned that while efficiency can lead to the camps of Auschwitz or the streets of Budapest, only the ideals of humanity and love can climb the hill to the Acropolis.

'A Rarer Commodity'

A third danger is timidity. Few men are willing to brave the disapproval of their fellows, the censure of their colleagues, the wrath of their society. Moral courage is a rarer commodity than bravery in battle or great intelligence. Yet it is the one essential, vital quality for those who seek to change a world that yields most painfully to change. Aristotle tells us that "at the Olympic games it is not the finest and the strongest men who are crowned, but they who enter the lists. . . . So too in the life of the honorable and the good it is they who act rightly who win the prize." I believe that in this generation those with the courage to enter the moral conflict will find themselves with companions in every corner of the world.

For the fortunate among us, the fourth danger is comfort, the temptation to follow the easy and familiar paths of personal ambition and financial success so grandly spread before those who enjoy the privilege of education. But that is not the road history has marked out for us. There is a Chinese curse that says, "May he live in interesting times." Like it or not, we live in interesting times. They are times of danger and uncertainty, but they are also more open to the creative energy of men than any other time in history. And all of us will ultimately be judged, and as the years pass we will surely judge ourselves, on the effort we have contributed to building a new world society and the extent to which our ideals and goals have shaped that effort.

Our future may lie beyond our vision, but it is not completely beyond our control. It is the shaping impulse of America that neither fate nor nature nor the irresistible tides of history, but the work of our own hands, matched to reason and principle, will determine our destiny. There is pride in that, even arrogance, but there is also experience and truth. In any event, it is the only way we can live.

Fordham University, June 10, 1967

'THE REVOLUTION
WITHIN OUR GATES'

*First as Attorney General and later as a Senator
and Presidential candidate, Robert Kennedy turned
his attention and commitment to the issues of civil
rights, of equal opportunity, and of racial equality:*

THE GREAT challenge before us is . . . the revolution within our gates, the struggle of Negro Americans for full equality and freedom. . . .

This will not be achieved by a law or a law-suit, by a single program, or in a single year. It means overcoming the scarred heritage of centuries of oppression, poor education, and the many obstacles to fruitful employment. It means dissolving ghettos—the physical ghettos of our big cities and those ghettos of the mind which separate white from black with hatred and ignorance, fear and mistrust. It means a revolution which has spread from the Deep South to the cities of the North—to every place, in fact, where black Americans seek to leap the gulf dividing them from the city of promise.

Some among us say the Negro has made great progress—which is true—and that he should be satisfied and patient—which is neither true nor realistic. In the past twenty years we have witnessed a revolution of rising expectations in almost every continent. That revolution has spread to the Negro nation confined within our own. Men without hope, resigned to despair and

'A revolution of rising expectations. . . .'

oppression, do not make revolutions. It is when expectation replaces submission, when despair is touched with the awareness of possibility, that the forces of human desire and the passion for justice are unlocked.

If we deny a man his place in the larger community, then he may turn inward to find his manhood and identity, rejecting those he feels have rejected him. Therefore, far more impressive than the violence of a few is the fact that the overwhelming majority of American Negroes retain their faith in the good will of the nation and the possibilities of peaceful progress within the ordered framework of American politics and life.

SOCIAL PROGRESS and social justice, in my judgment, are not something apart from freedom; they are the fulfillment of freedom. The obligation of free men is to use their opportunities to improve the welfare of their fellow human beings. This, at least, has been the tradition of democratic freedom in America. It will be the permanent effort of Americans to keep moving ever forward until we can realize the promise of American life for all our citizens.

IT SHOULD be clear that, if one man's rights are denied, the rights of all are in danger—that if one man is denied equal protection of the law, we cannot be sure that we will enjoy freedom of speech or any other of our fundamental rights.

History Has placed us all, black and white, within a common border and under a common law. All of us, from the wealthiest and most powerful of men to the weakest and hungriest of children, share one precious possession: the name "American." It is not easy to know what that means. But in part to be an American means to have been an outcast and a stranger, to have come to the exiles' country, and to know that he who denies the outcast and stranger among us at that moment also denies America.

ON EXTREMISM

Robert Kennedy had no patience with extremists from any quarter, knowing as he painfully and personally did the terrible consequences of hatred:

What Is objectionable, what is dangerous about extremists is not that they are extreme, but that they are intolerant. The evil is not what they say about their cause, but what they say about their opponents.

To Understand the causes [of riots] is not to permit the result. No man has the right to wantonly menace the safety and well-being of his neighbors. All citizens have the right to security in the streets of their community—in Birmingham or in Los Angeles. And it is the duty of all public officials to keep the public peace and bring to justice those who violate it. . . .

Cruelty and wanton violence may temporarily relieve a feeling of frustration, a sense of impotence. But the damage of those who perpetrate it—these are the negation of reason and the antithesis of humanity, and they are the besetting sins of the twentieth century.

Surely the world has seen enough, in the last forty years, of violence and hatred. Surely we have seen enough of the attempt to justify present injustice by past slights, or to punish the unjust by making the world more unjust.

We know now that the color of an executioner's robe matters little. And we know in our hearts, even through times of passion and discontent, that to add to the quantity of violence in this country is to burden our own lives, and mortgage our children's souls and the best possibilities of the American future.

EXTEMPORANEOUS EULOGY TO MARTIN LUTHER KING, JR.

Flying to Indianapolis, Robert Kennedy heard by radio of the assassination of Nobel Peace Prizewinner Dr. Martin Luther King, Jr. At the Indianapolis airport, the Senator delivered this extemporaneous eulogy:

DR. KING dedicated himself to justice and love between his fellow human beings. He gave his life for that principle and it is up to those who are here—his fellow citizens and public officials—to carry out that dream, to try to end the divisions that exist so deeply in our country and to remove the stain of bloodshed from our land.

Those of you who are black can be filled with bitterness, with hatred and a desire for revenge. We can move in that direction as a country, in greater polarization—black amongst black, white people amongst white, filled with hatred toward one another.

I had a member of my family killed. He was killed by a white man. But we have to make an effort in the United States—an effort to understand.

We can make an effort, as Martin Luther King did, to understand and to comprehend, and to replace violence with compassion and with love. What we need in the United States is love and wisdom and compassion toward one another, and a feeling of justice toward those who still suffer within our own country, whether they be white or they be black.

Aeschylus wrote: "In our sleep, pain that cannot forget falls drop by drop upon the heart and in our own despair, against our will, comes wisdom through the awful grace of God."

Let us dedicate ourselves to what the Greeks wrote so many years ago: to tame the savageness of men and make gentle the life of the world. Let us dedicate ourselves to that, and say a prayer for our country and for our people.

April 4, 1968

'BRIDGE ACROSS THE
GENERATIONS'

*To young people, Robert Kennedy spoke frankly and
with enthusiasm, as he does here in these excerpts
from speeches delivered in colleges across America:*

DEVOTED AND intelligent men have worked for generations to improve the well-being of the American people,
diminish poverty and injustice, and protect freedom.
Yet, even as we honor their accomplishments, we know
that our own problems will not yield to the ideas and
programs on which past achievement has been built.
Ideas are often more confining—more difficult to dis-
card—in their success than in their failure. Yet we must
cast aside many tested concepts in the face of challenges
whose nature and dimension are more complex and
towering than any before. For this, we must look to
your [younger] generation, a generation which feels
most intensely the agony and bewilderment of the
modern age and which is not bound to old ways of
thought.

THE GAP between generations will never be completely
closed. But it must be spanned. For the bridge across
the generations is essential to the nation in the present;
and more, it is the bridge to our own future—and thus
in a central sense, to the very meaning of our own lives.
Whatever their differences with us, whatever the depth
of their dissent, it is vital for us as much as for them

that our young feel that change is possible, that they will be heard, that the follies and cruelties of the world will yield, however grudgingly, to the sacrifices they are prepared to make. Above all, we seek a sense of possibility.

Possibility must begin with dialogue, which is more than the freedom to speak. It is the willingness to listen, and to act. To the extent that the young only mirror dissatisfactions common to their elders, they are raising matters that should concern us in any case. To the extent that they demand the observance of long-proclaimed ideals, they perform for us the ancient service of prophets. And as they ask for opportunities to contribute to mankind and shape their own fate, as so many have done in the Peace Corps, or in the Civil Rights movement, they lend greater urgency to a concern that all of us share: that our lives should make a difference to ourselves and our fellow men.

EVERY GENERATION has its central concern, whether to end war, erase racial injustice, or improve the condition of the working man. Today's young people appear to have chosen for their concern the dignity of the individual human being. They demand a limitation upon excessive power. They demand a political system that preserves the sense of community among men. They demand a government that speaks directly and honestly to its citizens. We can win their commitment only by demonstrating that these goals are possible through personal effort. The possibilities are too great, the stakes too high, to bequeath to the coming generation only the prophetic lament of Tennyson:

> Ah, what shall I be at fifty,
> Should nature keep me alive,
> If I find the world so bitter
> When I am but twenty-five?

WE MAY find that we learn most of all from those political and social dissenters whose differences with us are most grave; for among the young, as among adults, the sharpest criticism often goes hand in hand with the deepest idealism and love of country.

THE WAR IN VIETNAM
In 1967, after visiting Southeast Asia, Kennedy spoke trenchantly and with eloquence before the Senate about the continuing war in Vietnam. The speech began:

THE ASTOUNDING might of American power now falls upon a remote and alien people in a small and unknown land. It is difficult to feel in our hearts what this war means to Vietnam; it is on the other side of the world, and its people are strangers. Few of us are directly involved, while the rest of us continue our lives and pursue our ambitions undisturbed by the sounds and fears of battle. To the Vietnamese, however, it must often

'To know, to feel the burden of responsibility. . . .'

seem the fulfillment of the prophecy of Saint John the Divine: "And I looked, and beheld a pale horse: and his name that sat on him was Death, and Hell followed with him. And power was given unto them over the fourth part of the earth, to kill with sword, with hunger, and with death. . . ."

Although the world's imperfections may call forth the acts of war, righteousness cannot obscure the agony and pain those acts bring to a single child. The Vietnamese war is an event of historic moment, summoning the power and concern of many nations. But it is also the vacant moment of amazed fear as a mother and child watch death by fire fall from the improbable machine sent by a country they barely comprehend. It is the sudden terror of the official or the hamlet militiaman absorbed in the work of his village as he realizes the assassin is taking his life. It is the refugees wandering homeless from villages now obliterated, leaving behind only those who did not live to flee. It is the young men, Vietnamese and American, who in an instant sense the night of death destroying yesterday's promise of family and land and home. . . .

All we say and all we do must be informed by our awareness that this horror is partly our responsibility; not just a nation's responsibility but yours and mine. It is we who live in abundance and send our young men out to die. It is our chemicals that scorch the children and our bombs that level the villages. We are all participants. To know, to feel the burden of responsibility, is not to ignore the important interests, nor to forget that freedom and security must sometimes be paid for in blood. Still even though we must know as a nation what it is necessary to do, we must also feel as men the anguish of what it is we are doing.

When he published his Vietnam speech in his last book, To Seek a Newer World, *the Senator added a note discussing his personal responsibility for the war:* It may be that the effort [in Vietnam] was doomed from the start, that it was never really possible to bring all the people of South Vietnam under the rule of the successive governments we supported—governments, one after another, riddled with corruption, inefficiency, and greed; governments which did not and could not successfully capture and energize the national feeling of their people. If that is the case, as it well may be, then I am willing to bear my share of the responsibility, before my fellow-citizens. But past error is no excuse for its perpetuation. Tragedy is a tool for the living to gain wisdom, not a guide by which to live. Now as ever, we do ourselves best justice when we measure ourselves against ancient tests, as in the *Antigone* of Sophocles: "All men make mistakes, but a good man yields when he knows his course is wrong, and repairs the evil. The only sin is pride."

ON THE ARMS RACE

Tempered by the forging experience of the
Soviet-American confrontation over missiles in
Cuba, Robert Kennedy sought urgently to see
nuclear weapons contained and controlled:

THE NEED to halt the spread of nuclear weapons must be a central priority of American policy, deserving and demanding the greatest additional effort. Should nuclear weapons become generally available to the world . . . each crisis of the moment might well become the last crisis for all mankind.

The United States took the initiative and made the maximum effort to secure the nuclear test-ban treaty in 1963 because we knew that our security and the future of the world depended on halting the arms race and exerting every possible effort toward peace. But we have not yet taken the second step. The world has not moved, beyond the limited nuclear test ban itself, to halt the proliferation of nuclear weapons. At the onset of this journey, we cannot allow the demands of day-to-day policy, even on matters of serious importance, to obstruct our efforts to solve the problem of nuclear spread. We cannot wait for lasting peace in Southeast Asia, which will not come until nuclear weapons have spread beyond recall; nor for a general European settlement, which has not existed since 1914; nor until all nations learn to behave, for bad behavior armed with nuclear weapons is the danger we must try to prevent.

THE DESTRUCTION of the World Wars was limited only by technology. Now nuclear weapons have removed that limit. Who can say that they will not be used, that a rational balance of terror will restrain emotions we do not understand? . . . Nuclear war may never come, but it would be the rashest folly and ignorance to think that it will not come because men, being reasonable beings, will realize the destruction it would cause. . . .

This generation has unlocked the mystery of nature; henceforth all men must live with the power of complete self-destruction. This is the power of choice, the tragedy and glory of man. As Pope Paul has said, "The real danger comes from man himself." That is the hardest danger to avert. But it is the one we must face.

THE PROBLEM OF THE CITIES
Urban problems engaged Robert Kennedy
increasingly as he moved successively from
Attorney General to junior Senator from New York
to candidate for the Presidency:

THE SLUMS are a reality, as are idleness and poverty, lack of education and dilapidated housing. Frustrated expectations and disappointed hopes are realities. Above all, the awareness of injustice and the passion to end it are inescapable realities. Thus, we can face our difficulties and strive to overcome them, with imagination and dedication, wisdom and courage. Or we can turn away—bringing repression, steadily increasing human pain and civil strife, and leaving a problem of far more terrible and threatening proportions to our children.

THE TIME has come to stem the flow to the cities—to prevent their further sprawling over the landscape, their further oppression of men's souls. The time has come when we must actively fight bigness and overconcentration—and seek instead to bring the engines of government, of technology, of the economy, fully under the control of our citizens, to recapture and reinforce the values of a more human time and place.

IT WAS ATHENS, the very mother of cities, which showed us that greatness does not require size—even as others have shown us that size does not necessarily bring greatness.

THE CITY is not just housing and stores. It is not just education and employment, parks and theaters, banks and shops. It is a place where men should be able to live in dignity and security and harmony, where the great achievements of modern civilization and the ageless pleasures afforded by natural beauty should be available to all.

If this is what we want—and this is what we must want if men are to be free for the "pursuit of happiness" which was the earliest promise of the American nation

—we will need more than poverty programs, housing programs, and employment programs, although we will need all of these. We will need an outpouring of imagination, ingenuity, discipline and hard work unmatched since the first adventurers set out to conquer the wilderness. For the problem is the largest we have ever known. And we confront an urban wilderness more formidable and resistant and in some ways more frightening than the wilderness faced by the pilgrims or the pioneers.

BOTH CAUSE and consequence of all the rest [of the problems of cities] is the destruction of the sense, and often the fact, of community, of human dialogue—the thousand invisible strands of common experience and purpose, affection and respect, which tie men to their fellows. It is expressed in such words as community, neighborhood, civic pride, friendship. It provides the life-sustaining force of human warmth and security among others, and a sense of one's own human significance in the accepted association and companionship of others.

We all share things as fellow citizens, fellow members of the American nation.

As important as that sharing is, nations or great cities are too huge to provide the values of community. Community demands a place where people can see and know each other, where children can play and adults work together and join in the pleasures and responsibilities of the place where they live. The whole history of the human race, until today, has been the history of community. Yet this is disappearing—and disappearing at a time when its sustaining strength is badly needed.

'THE STAKE IS PERSONAL'

That individual energy and individual commitment could change the course of history Robert Kennedy never doubted. The influence of individuals was a compelling theme:

ONE HUNDRED years ago the test for the American people was whether the ideals and principles on which this Nation was created could be extended to all and still endure on this continent. Now, one hundred years later, the issues are relatively the same. The scope, however, is worldwide.

It is this enlargement of scope which accounts, I think, for much of the bafflement and confusion of our own time. The issues of the Civil War were vivid and immediate. The appeal to duty was plain. The involvement was personal. The response, on both sides, was unstinted and heroic.

But the enlargement of scale in the century since the Civil War has taken many issues out of the area of direct personal involvement and comprehension. Ours is a time when many things are just too big to be grasped. It is a century which has heaped up enough ex-

'To work out new ways of fulfilling our personal concern. . . .'

plosive power to blow up the world. It is a century which has probed into the floor of the sea, which has flung men far into outer space, which now threatens to invade the moon.

When things are done on too vast a scale, the human imagination bogs down. It can no longer visualize such fantastic things and thus loses its grip on their essential reality. Killing one man is murder; killing millions is a statistic. The disclosures of the Eichmann trial remind us all how quickly the world has forgotten the massive horrors which one set of human beings perpetrated against another a short twenty years ago.

Our problems, having grown to the size of the world, if not of the solar system, no longer seem our own. Each day we are required to respond to new crises created by people whose names we cannot pronounce in lands of which we have never heard. After a time, the capacity to respond begins to flag; and we turn, not cheerfully, but almost in despair, to the sports pages and the comics.

And yet I would say to you that the stake is just as personal today as it was a century ago, the obligation just as personal, the capacity to affect the course of history just as great. What we require is not the self-indulgence of resignation from the world but the hard effort to work out new ways of fulfilling our personal concern and our personal responsibility.

[President Kennedy] has said: "Ask not what your country can do for you—ask what you can do for your country." And many writers have said: "Tell us, Mr. President, tell the American people and they will do it."

I think myself that if we have to wait to be told we are indeed in a bad way.

Some of us, I fear, think of sacrifice as a big, once-and-for-all gesture, something dramatic, gratifying—and falling in the main on somebody else.

But the real point about sacrifice, except in times of open warfare, is surely that it tends to be undramatic, prolonged and irritating.

When you have a democratic system in which every view can be expressed, there is also a great responsibility imposed on the individual. This is a tremendous freedom that has been granted us. But we have to have the responsibility to exercise it properly.

The answer is not violence against those who disagree. The answer is to have the courage of your convictions and be willing to stand up and be counted. It doesn't do any good to retreat within yourselves and just exchange views with those who already agree with you and yell slogans and march with signs. Something more is required of people who live in a democratic system.

No citizen can escape from freedom and still enjoy it. We cannot corrupt our own processes of government and law nor allow others to do so. We cannot yield to the temptation to let someone else perform the job, or to remain aloof from what in a free society is every-body's business.

SINCE THE days of Greece and Rome when the word "citizen" was a title of honor, we have often seen more emphasis put on the rights of citizenship than on its responsibilities. And today, as never before in the free world, responsibility is the greatest right of citizenship and service is the greatest of freedom's privileges.

ALL GREAT questions must be raised by great voices, and the greatest voice is the voice of the people—speaking out—in prose, or painting, or poetry, or music; speaking out—in homes and halls, streets and farms, courts and cafes—let that voice speak and the stillness you hear will be the gratitude of mankind.

SUCCESS IN international affairs, no less than in domestic matters, depends on active interest and support not only by our leaders but by all of us. The responsibility of world power, like that of democracy, is something that must be shared by all citizens of the nation that enjoys it—citizens who know how much they have to gain by sustaining it, and how much they have to lose if it should ever fail.

LET NO man think he fights his battle for others. He fights for himself and so do we all. The golden rule is not sentimentality, but the deepest practical wisdom.

48

For the teaching of our time is that cruelty is contagious and its disease knows no bounds of race or nation.

IN THE LAST analysis every issue comes at last to a set of intellectual and moral decisions within the mind and heart of each one of us as individuals.

My experience every day . . . reinforces my conviction that our democracy will stand or fall on the capacity of each individual in the nation to meet his responsibilities.

Most of our fellow citizens do their best—and do it the modest, unspectacular, decent, natural way which is the highest form of public service.

THE ADVENTURE OF CHANGE
*As it had been for his brother, change was a
subject of major interest to Robert Kennedy. He
spoke often of its problems and promises:*

THE ADVENTURE of change may be a tragic adventure for many—a sad uprooting of cherished customs and institutions. Yet change is the one constant of history. It has certainly been the dominating fact in the development of my own country. From the first moment of independence, the United States has been dedicated to innovation as a way of government and a way of life. Not a decade has gone by in our nation's history in which we did not undergo new experiences and see new challenges. We were born in a revolution against colonialism, and we have been dedicated ever since to a revolution for freedom and progress.

WE ARE a nation which has reached the height of its power and influence at a time when the old order of things is crumbling and the new world is painfully struggling to take shape. It is a moment as fully charged with opportunity as that granted to Columbus or the heroes of the Italian Renaissance. It offers to this nation the chance for great achievement—or perhaps the greatest and most destructive of failures. . . . The way is uncertain, and the trip is charged with hazard. Yet perhaps we can say, in the words of Garibaldi to his followers: "I do not promise you ease. I do not promise you comfort. But I do promise you these: hardship, weariness, and suffering. And with them, I promise you victory."

WE HAVE not solved our problems, but we are committed to find solutions. And most important, the country has turned away, I hope forever, from those whose hearts are dry as summer dust, those who feel that the poor are evil, that security is weakening, and that every man should fend for himself.

IF WE fail to dare, if we do not try, the next generation will harvest the fruit of our indifference; a world we did not want—a world we did not choose—but a world we could have made better, by caring more for the results of our labors. And we shall be left only with the hollow apology of T. S. Eliot:

"That is not what I meant at all.

"That is not it, at all."

EVERY MAN must have his own vision of things to come. But many Americans, I believe, share broad and deep hopes for the world—the hope of a world without war —of a world where peoples now suffering in poverty and oppression can win a better life for themselves and their children—of a world where the imagination and energy of mankind are dedicated, not to destruction, but to building a generous and spacious future.

And many Americans too, I think, share broad and deep hopes for our own land—and hope of a land in which every child born has a decent opportunity for education, medical care and employment—of a land where intolerance and segregation become a memory, and a Negro child born in a cotton field in Alabama is as secure in his rights as a white child born here in Washington—of a land where poverty is a thing of the past, and every American has a free and equal chance to realize his own individual talent and possibilities.

If this is the vision of the future—if this is the direction in which we want to move—the next thing we must consider is how we propose to get there, and what obstacles lie in our path. For such a vision is never self-fulfilling. We cannot stand idly by and expect our

'The future is not a gift: it is an achievement.'

dreams to come true under their own power. The future is not a gift: it is an achievement. Every generation helps make its own future. This is the essential challenge of the present. A hundred years from now there will be new ways of making life better, of giving man fuller opportunity to fulfill his hopes.

We have no infallible party, no iron creed, no all-purpose blueprint; we do not propose to chain mankind to a system of false logic. We have instead faith in human intelligence, human will and human decency; and we know that, in the long run, these are the forces which make history.

THE CHALLENGE OF COMMUNISM
To confront Communism, Robert Kennedy raised the challenge of the open, free society, and he found in America the true fulfillment of the old revolutionary dream. It was a theme he returned to again and again:

THE HISTORY of America—and, in fact, America today —is full of men and ideas that are far more exciting and revolutionary than the systematic, pushbutton answers of Communist doctrine. I would like to see more Americans making this point. By not doing so, we are leaving most of the world with the illusion that the only modern philosophy belongs to Marx. Mere anti-Communism is not a philosophy; it is no substitute for really knowing what this country is about. Its history, its philosophy, its political thought are all available. They just need to be used.

We Must make very clear the basic distinction between Communism and the Free World; that we are the heirs of the true revolution that will not accept the *status quo* and recognizes that the state exists for the individual and that the individual is not the servant of the state; that we live by the rule of law with all its fundamental guarantees that the truth will be known and that individual citizens will be protected from injustice and tyranny.

Every American knows in his heart of the truth of the democratic way of life. But a nice warm feeling in the heart doesn't take the place of knowing what he's talking about. . . .

The challenge is whether we as a people and a nation can demonstrate it. The struggle . . . can be won—but it also can be lost. The decision is ours.

Communism Everywhere has paid the price of rigidity and dogmatism. Freedom has the strength of compassion and flexibility. It has, above all, the strength of intellectual honesty. We do not claim to know all the answers; we make no pretense of infallibility. And we know this to be a sign, not of weakness, but of power.

The proof of the power of freedom lies in the fact that Communism has always flinched from competition in the field where it counts most—the competition of ideas. . . .

We proudly press the challenge: let the ideas of freedom have the same circulation in Communist states that Communist ideas have in free states. We can have formal peace without such reciprocal competition in the realm of ideas; but until we have full freedom of intellectual exchange, I see no prospect of a genuine and final relaxation of world tension.

MARX's CONDEMNATION of the heartless laissez-faire capitalism of the early nineteenth century now—by an irony of history—applies with fantastic precision to twentieth-century Communism. . . .

It is Communism, not free society, which has become the favorite twentieth-century means of disciplining the masses, repressing consumption and denying the workers the full produce of their labor.

By this historical paradox, it is free society, and not Communism, which seems most likely to realize Marx's old hope of the emancipation of man and the achievement of an age of universal abundance.

HISTORY Is a relentless master. It has no present, only the past rushing into the future. To try to hold fast is to be swept aside.

LET Us never forget that we are the descendants of the greatest revolutionaries the world has ever known.

'I feel that I'm obliged to do all that I can.'

ANNOUNCEMENT OF
PRESIDENTIAL CANDIDACY

*On Saturday, March 16, 1968, in the same room in
the Senate Office Building where, eight years
earlier, his brother John had announced his
candidacy, Robert Kennedy entered the race for
the Presidency of the United States:*

I AM announcing today my candidacy for the Presidency of the United States.

I do not run for the Presidency merely to oppose any man but to propose new policies. I run because I am convinced that this country is on a perilous course and because I have such strong feelings about what must be done, and I feel that I'm obliged to do all that I can.

I run to seek new policies—policies to end the bloodshed in Vietnam and in our cities, policies to close the gap that now exists between black and white, between rich and poor, between young and old in this country and around the rest of the world.

I run for the Presidency because I want the Democratic party and the United States of America to stand for hope instead of despair, for reconciliation of men instead of the growing risk of world war. . . .

No one who knows what I know about the extraordinary demands of the Presidency can be certain that any mortal can adequately fill that position.

But my service on the National Security Council during the Cuban missile crisis, the Berlin crisis of 1961 and 1962 and later, the negotiations on Laos and on the nuclear test ban treaty have taught me something about both the uses and the limitations of military power, about the value of negotiations with allies and with enemies, about the opportunities and dangers which await our nation in many corners of the globe in which I have traveled.

As a member of the Cabinet and a member of the Senate I have seen the inexcusable and ugly deprivations which cause children to starve in Mississippi, black citizens to riot in Watts, young Indians to commit suicide on their reservations because they've lacked all hope and they feel they have no future, and proud and able-bodied families to wait out their lives in empty idleness in eastern Kentucky.

I have traveled and I have listened to the people of our nation and felt their anger about the war that they are sent to fight and about the world that they are about to inherit. . . .

I do not lightly dismiss the dangers and the difficulties of challenging an incumbent President. But these are not ordinary times and this is not an ordinary election. ⸺

At stake is not simply the leadership of our party and even our country. It is our right to the moral leadership of this planet.

EULOGY TO ROBERT F. KENNEDY
At St. Patrick's Cathedral in New York, on June
8, 1968, Senator Edward M. Kennedy delivered
this eulogy to his slain brother:

YOUR EMINENCES, Your Excellencies, Mr. President. In behalf of Mrs. Kennedy, her children, the parents and sisters of Robert Kennedy, I want to express what we feel to those who mourn with us today in this cathedral and around the world.

We loved him as a brother and as a father and as a son. From his parents and from his older brothers and sisters, Joe and Kathleen and Jack, he received an inspiration which he passed on to all of us.

He gave us strength in time of trouble, wisdom in time of uncertainty and sharing in time of happiness. He will always be by our side.

Love is not an easy feeling to put into words. Nor is loyalty or trust or joy. But he was all of these. He loved life completely and he lived it intensely.

A few years back Robert Kennedy wrote some words about his own father which express the way we in his family felt about him. He said of what his father meant to him, and I quote:

"What it really all adds up to is love. Not love as it is described with such facility in popular magazines, but the kind of love that is affection and respect, order and encouragement and support.

"Our awareness of this was an incalculable source of

strength. And because real love is something unselfish and involves sacrifice and giving, we could not help but profit from it."

And he continued:

"Beneath it all he has tried to engender a social conscience. There were wrongs which needed attention, there were people who were poor and needed help, and we have a responsibility to them and this country.

"Through no virtues and accomplishments of our own, we have been fortunate enough to be born in the United States under the most comfortable conditions. We therefore have a responsibility to others who are less well off."

That is what Robert Kennedy was given.

What he leaves to us is what he said, what he did, and what he stood for. . . .

My brother need not be idealized or enlarged in death beyond what he was in life. He should be remembered simply as a good and decent man who saw wrong and tried to right it, saw suffering and tried to heal it, saw war and tried to stop it.

Those of us who loved him and who take him to his rest today pray that what he was to us, and what he wished for others, will someday come to pass for all the world.

As he said many times, in many parts of this nation, to those he touched and who sought to touch him:

"Some men see things as they are and say, why. I dream things that never were and say, why not."

ROBERT F. KENNEDY'S LIFE—
A CHRONOLOGY

1925 Born November 20, Brookline, Massachusetts, to Joseph P. and Rose Kennedy, their seventh child and third son.

1948 Graduated from Harvard College.

1950 Married to Ethel Skakel.

1951 Graduated from University of Virginia Law School. Began work in Justice Department.

1952 Managed John F. Kennedy's Senate campaign.

1953 For six months, served as counsel to the Senate Permanent Investigations Subcommittee, headed by Senator Joseph McCarthy. Resigned.

1955 Became chief counsel to the Senate Permanent Investigations Subcommittee, now headed by Senator John McClellan.

1960 Managed John F. Kennedy's successful campaign for the Presidency and was appointed Attorney General of the new Administration.

1963 President John F. Kennedy assassinated, November 22.

1964 Resigned as Attorney General to run for Senator from New York, and was elected.

1968 Announced Presidential candidacy in March. Assassinated in Los Angeles after victory in California primary; died June 6 at age 42.

Set in Linotype Aldus, a roman with old-face
characteristics, designed by Hermann Zapf.
Aldus was named for the 16th century Venetian
printer Aldus Manutius.
Typography by Grant Dahlstrom, set at
The Castle Press.
Printed on Hallmark Eggshell Book paper.
Designed by Harald Peter.